Week 1

#1: Write out your ideal interest group persona

Your mission starts here.

List down the particular fragments of individuals that you are focusing at. The stunt here is to not be general but not barely unambiguous with portraying these customers.

Let's say you have an imaginative thought for focus point lunch box suppers. 'Individuals who like to eat' are too expansive a class, while 'Individuals who like to eat just spaghetti bolognese with hamburger' is excessively thin. 'Middle class laborers who work in the city and focus point their day to day lunch from inexpensive food chains' sounds much better.

Then, you'll have to make reasonable deductions to figure out what their most serious issues are, and what they need the most. I have observed that it helps hugely to foster client personas, which are made up models of your objective customer.

A fast and basic method for doing this is to go to the roads and ask 10 individuals who fit your interest group profile. Assuming they raise the very issues that you speculated and are effectively searching for arrangements, you have a triumphant campaign.

You get the idea.

#2: Write out the 3 guiding principle recommendations of your product

In 30 seconds, you should have the option to rattle off in list item length, not multiple ways that your clients' lives will improve by utilizing your item. You ought to likewise have the option to depict how you predict your client involving your item in their regular routines, and under specific occasions or scenarios.

#3: Decide on an appealing name for your product

Take time here to painstakingly figure what you'll need to name your item. When your item name is out there on the lookout, it sticks to people groups like superglue.

My startup group and I endured fourteen days conceptualizing and agonizing, and bantering over an able name for what might become 'Two part harmony: The Smart Bluetooth Tag'. You might have a hard time believing it, yet we got going with exhausting or absurd sounding names like "Tag", "Peach", "Tango", before one brilliant person proposed "Two part harmony", since the gadget safeguards two things at once.

It helps immensely to do a speedy survey of item names with your loved ones, and request them their thought process from every item when it is referenced to them.

#4: Decide on the crowdfunding stage you'll need to use

Really, settling on your crowdfunding site of decision ought not be intense by any means. But before you start drowning in the sea of crowdfunding sites, the first thing you'll want to do is to write down your goals: How much do you want to raise etc. Then, research about crowdfunding sites which are most conducive for your product. Kickstarter and Indiegogo turn out extraordinary for creatives, film and tech projects. GoFundMe is great for gifts, while MedStartr is taken care of the clinical business. Observe that practically all stages charge 5-6% of your assets raised.

For a more in-depth guide to choosing crowdfunding sites, check out my other book: 'How To Choose A Crowdfunding Site'.

#5: Decide on the financing objective and mission length

This is one of those significant, represent the moment of truth questions you should ask yourself. A financing objective that is set too high could mean gambling with long periods of difficult work and leaving with no capital, assuming you are utilizing a 'fixed subsidizing' campaign.

On the other hand, an objective set too low could imply that you need to foot extra mission costs out of your own pocket, an exorbitant move you would rather not make.

Before you decide on a funding figure, here are three battle-tried, suggestions I'll make:

1. Start by totalling all undertaking and award satisfaction costs

2. Budget for more cash than you suspect you'll need

3. Always put forth your financing objective lower than what you need

#6: Setup the vital ledgers/installment processors (Amazon Payments in the event that utilizing Kickstarter)

If you're crowdfunding on Kickstarter, you MUST have an Amazon Payments account. Kickstarter requires project makers to confirm their character through an Amazon Payments business account, an interaction that can take more time to seven days. The limitations kick in here, since you'll have to have a US address and financial balance to fit the bill for Amazon Payments. You'll need to enroll for a US address and ledger in the event that you don't have one.

The other option, obviously, is register your Kickstarter project under a US resident's name all things considered, and have the person in question set up an Amazon Payments represent you. That is expecting you have a companion or a contact that is a US resident, and will help you out.

For Indiegogo, all you want is a PayPal Business record and you're all set. For any remaining locales, read their installment necessities carefully.

#7: Create a pre-crusade greeting page with an email interest select in structure on Launchrock

Creating adequate buzz prior to sending off your crowdfunding effort is super significant! You can create whiz around your item regardless of whether your mission isn't prepared at this point. Direct people to your site point of arrival, and capture emails using launchrock.com. Launchrock allows you to set up a point of arrival shortly and is exceptionally easy to utilize. Best of all, it's completely free!

*Power tip: Have a giveaway promotion to boost individuals to information exchange for your item send off. We ran a reference challenge to give out 10 Duet gadgets to 10 fortunate folks, and we received 400 leads consequently. Individuals truly love free stuff!

#8: Setup a free email promoting account with Mailchimp

Mailchimp is an email advertising programming that makes it simple to plan messages to be conveyed to your list.

You'll require a method for keeping in contact with your endorsers and keep them locked in. On the off chance that you don't remain in consistent contact with your email records for over a month, they will begin to develop cold. That is the reason you ought to have Mailchimp to robotize this interaction for you. All you really want is to set up a straightforward succession of autoresponder messages, something like this:

Email 1: Welcome and a debt of gratitude is in order for

your advantage! - At information exchange Email 2: Our

account of how we got everything rolling - multi week after

the fact Email 3: When we are sending off - two weeks later

Email 4: Our mission dispatches today! - send off day

Tip: The less extravagant, less complex and more customized the email content, the better. Don't bother getting impeded by whimsical illustrations/formats. As I would like to think, the unassuming and past all text email works best, in an uproarious reality where organizations are attempting to offer things to us each and every day.

#9: Find out and incorporate a rundown of where your interest group hangs out online

Knowing where your crowd hangs out online is critical for your PR procedure later on. In the event that you don't have the foggiest idea where they hang out, you risk sending off your mission to some unacceptable group, or most exceedingly terrible nobody at all!

Start by asking yourself what web journals, sites, online networks, gatherings, vested parties are your main interest group liable to hang out in. On the off chance that you're focusing on business visionaries, Hacker News and TechCrunch will be their logical home base spots. In the event that you're taking a gander at equipment aficionados, Good.is

is another extraordinary community.

Compile every one of these home base puts into a rundown and extra to it as you find more sources. You ought to do this from the get-go in your mission, as it takes more time to sort out these places.

#10: Promote your point of arrival by and by email to your family and dear friends

You want an affection to get everything rolling. Your loved ones are your most prominent venture allies, thus you'll need to allow them to be quick to realize that you're leaving on this invigorating project!

Send every one of them a customized email, asking them to information exchange for refreshes when your mission is going to be sent off. It's essential to address them each by name, instead of a conventional 'Dear Family'. Individuals are more able to make a move when mentioned as people, as opposed to as a group.

#11: Start searching for an inventive video organization (paid option)

Your mission video is the best foot forward at persuading individuals to promise to your undertaking. So search for an expert or a respectable video office that can shoot and alter a top notch video.

In my perspective, your video ought to be your greatest use, as it is your most noteworthy showcasing resource. A good video will serve you well in terms of sales for a long time to come. Besides, you can likewise reuse that equivalent video for different advancements, even after the mission has ended.

If you can bear the cost of it, pay the individual shooting your video well, and you'll be compensated with superior grade. The individual who created my video did a really brilliant work, and I'll absolutely love to impart to you her contact.

Just email me at johnathan@crowdfundedkit.com

Power tip: Your selection of entertainers/entertainers in your video is critical. Their nationality and skin tone ought to mirror the group that you are focusing on. For our crowdfunding effort, we had a mix of Western and
Asian groups, so we drew in a British-White male and a Singaporean-Eurasian female for our principle leads.

In a comparable vein, the voiceover craftsman you decide for your video ought to likewise match your objective audience.

#12: Start searching for a picture taker (paid option)

Again, very much like the video, don't hold back on the nature of your item illustrations. Chase around after a decent photographic artist to snap quality photos of your item. Guarantee that the photograph goals are sharp and clear. At the absolute minimum, have your chances finished with a DSLR camera.

Most of the time, individuals who do your video likewise have great associations with incredible photographic artists, as the inventive local area is firmly knitted.

Again, I have extraordinary contacts that shoot extraordinary photographs. Essentially drop me an email.

Week 2

#13: Brainstorm storyboard for item video

The primary thing before you shoot a video is to make a storyboard so you can rejuvenate your content and present it to others. A video storyboard is a progression of thumbnails that show the breakdown of the video, delineating the key scenes - how the setting will look, who will be available, and what moves will make place.

It is an extraordinary conceptualizing procedure to create thoughts. Utilizing pictorial delineations drawn on paper, you can rapidly maneuver your conceptualized video thoughts toward the ideal sequence.

Keep the storyboard straightforward: I just sketch my storyboard on paper, and by a long shot it is as yet the quickest method for reconsidering and make changes. It is extremely useful now to go through your video storyboard with whoever is shooting the video.

To start with storyboarding, first get a lot of hued markers and bits of plain paper (you will draw a lot of pictures). Then the principal thing to do before you draw out your scenes on paper is to ask yourself these questions:

- What is the objective of your item video?

- How should my item story be told?

- What individuals/situations ought to be displayed in the video?

Brainstorm and evoke as numerous scenes in your psyche in light of those three inquiries, and draw them out in pictures. The main rule you'll need to see in storyboarding is that each piece of paper can have one situation drawn on it. But do not limit or 'shoot down' any idea here, as doing so might stifle your creative juices. On the off chance that you would be able, glue up your bits of paper on a divider with tape.

Once you've conceptualized somewhere around 20 scenes, now is the right time to sift them through by

pertinence. Are the scenes you just conceptualized lined up with the 3 inquiries referenced before? Great. Fend them and lose all else.

The last advance would then be to grouping your thoughts in a consistent way that an individual can without much of a stretch comprehend. To provide you with an illustration of a video storyboard sequence:

Scene #1: Alan, an understudy is displayed in the garden

Scene #2: He exhibits how he utilizes his telephone to monitor schedule items

Scene #3: Alan snaps a photo with his sweetheart at a party

Scene #4: Alan lets us know he generally dislikes losing phones

Scene #5: Alan is shown running for a leaving taxi. He has left his telephone in there

Scene #6: He unintentionally thumps his telephone off a bistro table without understanding. Scene #7: Alan shows that he is extremely baffled with himself

Scene #8: Alan clutches the Duet and presses it

Scene #9: The Duet gadget rings Alan's phone.

Scene #10: Alan observes his telephone in twofold fast time.

#14: Plan crusade reward advantages and pricing

Rewards are benefits your supporters will receive as a trade-off for promising to your mission. For most of ventures, the principle rewards are generally early forms of the item itself.

The critical thing to recall as you plan your award advantages is to think in the shoes of your sponsor: "How might this benefit me?" This is an ideal opportunity to be innovative, and offer your benefactors compensates other than the center item or administration offering.

There are 3 accepted procedures I've found function admirably while arranging rewards:

1. Go for unmistakable advantages over elusive perks

2. Have a $1 token advantage for individuals to show support

3. Have a timely riser perk

Pricing wise, it is more craftsmanship than science. Regularly, the best rewards are between the $19-$50 territory. But if it's a tech or hardware product, then it's really fine for the price to be even higher. As evaluating can be very perplexing, the most ideal way to settle on what cost to set is to do a fast examination of comparative crowdfunding activities, and afterward utilize those costs as a benchmark.

#15: Plan a reference crusade for supporters to allude individuals to your site

With the right motivators, references are probably the most ideal way to produce a tremendous surge of sponsor promises. Assuming that you've shopped on Amazon.com previously, you could have acknowledged how strong the force of proposals can be.
Therefore, plan in advance for a reference crusade where your sponsor can allude their companions to your site.

One strategy for running a reference challenge is what I call the Refund Credits strategy. Permit me to take a leaf from the GOKey Indiegogo mission to figure out how this basic strategy works.

View the GOKey Campaign here

First, GOKey is a thin, conservative keychain adornment that has four helpful things in one: reinforcement charger, record sync link, streak drive and Bluetooth finder. The Indiegogo project raised an astounding $1,032,168, far unbelievable its subsidizing objective of $40,000.

The thought here is that assuming you are a GOKey sponsor, and like the item and need to assist with getting the news out, and anybody gets a GOKey because of you, GOKey will show its appreciation to you by crediting a $10 discount on your vow for every individual that purchases. So assuming you allude 6 companions and they purchase, you've actually returned any amount of money that is possible, and get your GOKey free of charge ($59 value).

Now who wouldn't be drawn to a free GOKey?

#16: Run Facebook Ads to drive traffic revenue to presentation page (paid option)

I am aware of no other instrument to get leads quicker than Facebook Ads. It is economical, and the most amazing aspect of utilizing Facebook Ads is that you can penetrate down to your ideal objective gathering. You can even 'slice and dice' the demographics by factors such as age, country, interests etc. So for instance, assuming you're attempting to get leads for another equipment item, your ideal interest group could be:

- Males between 25-55 years old
- Based in U.S, California
- Have an interest in customer electronics
- Are early tech adopters

Our mission accumulated an aggregate of 400 leads just from a giveaway challenge on the point of arrival. Absolute expense: $300. That works out to an expense of just $0.75 per lead. Not excessively bad!

#17: Promote your point of arrival in internet based networks where your ideal interest group hangs out

This is one more method for getting information exchanges rapidly. Recollect the rundown you've arranged in Step #9? This is the place where it comes in truly handy.

But advance with class: you would rather not seem to be one of those deceitful sales reps who just savage discussions with ads. The thoughtful method for advancing your greeting page is to first be a supporter in quite a while, and assemble trust. The brilliant decide that I follow is that until I've offered 20 accommodating posts or remarks, I won't specify anything by any stretch of the imagination about my impending campaign.

#18: Continue elevating your presentation page to your networks

Throughout the course of the week, you're probably going to interface with more individuals, both on the web and disconnected. Normally, you'll be eager to inform them concerning your impending effort. Make a move to allude them to your arrival page.

#19: Find out and compile a list of horizontal segments in your industry to promote (etc. university community mailing lists, industry watch mailing lists)

Beyond advancement to your own organizations and in web-based networks, you can likewise use on industry and college mailing records. There are a lot of email list proprietors who run huge email records, and you can reach them and solicitation for them to pitch your campaign.

Just to show to you how strong utilizing on college mailing records can be for prelaunch promotion:

In my past startup job, my originator and I turned out to be graduated class from the Singapore Management University. What we did was contact our guides over in the business division and mentioned their assistance to impact a college wide EDM illuminating understudies that we were setting up a stall nearby. They thoughtfully concurred, and what happened from there on was nothing kind of remarkable: on the day we showed up to arrangement our corner, we previously had 3 understudies enthusiastically sitting tight for us! Throughout the two days, understudies dropped by the droves. Before the finish of the 2-day crusade, we had assembled north of 80 intrigued leads for our mission launch.

That is the force of advancing your task offline!

#20: Send out email updates to your mailing list

Send an email to thank your rundown for showing their advantage in your mission. You ought to likewise impart obviously to them again what your crowdfunding effort is about, and make it unequivocally clear when your designated day for kickoff will be so they won't be surprised.

Week 3

#21: Refine video storyboard idea for video further

Continue dealing with adding more scenes to your storyboard. Eliminate those that don't check out, and start to give your characters names. Run the storyboard through with 2 or 3 others to check whether it makes sense.

#22: Start taking decent photos of your item prototype

Back to #12, it is currently time to make a move. Welcome your picture taker to your office to shoot the photographs (or do it without anyone's help on the off chance that you're a pro).

Power Tip: You don't have to have a completely working item to start shooting the photographs. All you'll require is to have essentially the external packaging prepared. We 3D-printed our model for our photograph shoot simply seven days earlier, and splash painted it to look credible. The point here is to improvise!

#23: Promote your presentation page to level industry segments

As referenced in Step #19, this is the best time for you to elevate your greeting page to the rundown of flat industry portions you've collected.

#24: Promote your greeting page on connect locales (Reddit, Hacker News etc.)

The following simple thing to do is to present your presentation page to interface casting a ballot or week after week email records. Regardless of whether your post hit the landing page of Hacker News, it might in any case get a little traffic from being on the new page.

Find the locales generally pertinent to your theme. Here are interface destinations you can begin with:

- Hacker News
- Reddit (there are subreddits on nearly every topic)
- Inbound.org
- Digg
- BetaLi.st
- GrowthHackers

#25: Start working out your composed pitch duplicate for crusade

The composed pitch expands upon your video pitch to assist with selling your mission. Consider it a subsequent advertising guarantee that extends and builds up your video pitch. After someone has watched the video, your pitch then continues to share further details to convince your viewer to pledge. Your ultimate objective is to have each watcher thinking: "Goodness! This person can guess what I might be thinking!" in the wake of perusing your pitch duplicate. In the event that you can convey the very agonies that your guests are feeling, you've nailed it!

Things you ought to expound on in your mission pitch:

- What the item is
- The tale of how your item came about
- Key advantages of your item to viewers
- Graphics and photos
- Social confirmation (from press inclusion, tributes etc.)
- Features of your product
- Pricing of your advantage packages
- Who your group is
- What will your assets be utilized for
- Risks and challenges
- FAQs

#26: Start collecting a rundown of significant media contacts for pitching your campaign

If you need your crowdfunding effort to truly succeed, its not to the point of just raising assets from your loved ones. You'll need to have more extensive inclusion in the media. Pretty much every mission that is raised more than $100,000 expected to have PR to assist with raising that degree of funds.

However, conventional PR organizations are typically not appropriate for new companies, particularly since their administrations can get truly costly. But the good news is that by using a couple of free online tools, you can still get PR coverage cost- effectively on your own and achieve the same (if not better) results than engaging a PR firm. The best part is that these tools do not cost you a single

dime. They make the most common way of reaching news sources a lot less

complex. Here they are:

- Buzzstream is a great tool to help you save time getting influential bloggers contact info

- Use Google Images to find media outlets that previously covered your competitors

- Kicktraq is a Kickstarter focused only tool to find media outlets that previously covered your competitors.

- Help A Reporter Out is a free service you can use to turn any journalist into your ally

However, this is as yet an extremely sluggish approach to gathering your rundown of contacts into one spot. On the other hand, you could buy media records containing names of the top bloggers, writers, journalists, and editors in your specialty. These rundowns likewise incorporate telephone numbers, direct email addresses, and bio data on them, so you can pitch them on your mission all the more really. Assuming you might want to buy one of these rundowns, drop me an email at johnathan@crowdfundedkit.com and I'll work something out for you.

If you would like further hands-on video training, check out the Startup Crowdfunding Udemy course that will teach you exactly how to use those tools.

Week 4

#27: Shoot the video

For me, this was the most astonishing movement in the whole crowdfunding process. For a couple of days, you'll feel like a Hollywood chief, just that somebody is coordinating and accomplishing basically everything for you. It's additionally energizing to hang tight for the main cut of the video as it is being produced.

Usually, the video shoot will require an entire little while. In the event that it is conceivable, head down along with the videographer to where the shoot is occurring. This is significant in light of the fact that then you can illuminate the chief to make changes on the spot, on the off chance that the video isn't going as indicated by your ideal taste.

#28: Create a transitory secret site for your product

Rather than pointing individuals straightforwardly to your Kickstarter or Indiegogo crusade page, which is very verbose, make a mystery site for your item. An engaging and straightforward page would function as an approach to getting the point about what you bring to the table across quickly.

Don't have to stress over programming abilities here. Unbounce.com is a great tool to help you set up beautiful, and high-converting teaser pages in just a matter of minutes.

#29: Finish composing your composed mission pitch

Your first draft of the mission pitch ought to be prepared now. Prior to finishing the pitch, have undoubtedly 2 different people to go through it and feature any syntactic slip-ups and give feedback.

#30: Find a rundown of disconnected spots to spread awareness

Promoting your mission disconnected is as yet perhaps the most effective way to get individuals inspired by your mission. That is on the grounds that nothing demonstrates the legitimacy of your mission in excess of an up close and personal conversation.

Some instances of disconnected places that you can advance are: meetup groups,
organizing occasions, classes, talks you give, and yes even Starbucks (seriously!).

#31: Prepare PR Press Kit for press coverage

Your press pack is the all in one resource for columnists and correspondents hoping to expound on your company.

When you are pitching to columnists and columnists with your story, it is critical to make it as simple as workable for them to expound on you. These individuals are continuously chipping away at tight cutoff times, and on such a large number of things.

Here are a critical things to remember for your press kit:

- Bios: Use this part to discuss your organization's authors, CEO, administrator, financial backers or some other key players.

- Press Releases: these are composed proclamations to the media declaring your newsworthy crowdfunding effort. Journalists are normally bound to think about a story thought assuming they initially get a public statement. Ensure that your mission day for kickoff is masterful obviously in the press release!

- Product Images: give high-res item photographs of your item that news sources can without much of a stretch use. You ought to likewise clarify that writers are permitted to republish the pictures or video with any fitting credits. Counting your organization logo here is a decent method for making your mission 'stay' with the public.

- Contact data: now and then individuals totally ignore this part. Furthermore, thusly, columnists have no real way to get in touch with them. List telephone numbers, and email addresses for your organization's representative, or assigned staff.

- Reviewer Guide (discretionary): remembering an analyst's aide for your press unit will separate your mission. The analyst's aide is a guidance manual that correspondents can use to arrangement and finish your product.

Once you have your press pack together, zip it up together into an envelope, or

transfer it on Dropbox and keep the 'shareable' interface handy.

For an illustration of a decent press unit, look at Ambiclimate's press kit:
<u>Ambiclimate press kit</u>
Week 5

#32: Review and alter first draft of video

I know. It is an exceptionally thrilling encounter to see the principal draft of your video in your email inbox. 99.99% of the time, you will in any case need to make alters to the main draft, before it is prepared for production.

What you ought to truly focus on for the primary draft of your video is to guarantee that the storyboard scenes are right, and that your item idea is plainly shown. So the primary thing you ought to do is to play the video a few times, and afterward contrast it back and the storyboard you had arranged before. Pay special attention to any missing scenes.

Check to guarantee that the lighting is correct and sound is clear and sufficiently uproarious. Yet, don't stress a lot over getting every one of these consummated at this point.

Those things will be settled when you get your last draft.

#33: Continue work on the brief mystery website

Resume work on your secret webpage. At this crossroads, your site ought to as of now have the majority of the substance up. This is an ideal opportunity to include illustrations and recordings, and furthermore to twofold make sure that your greeting page interfaces accurately to your mission page.

#34: Send out PR Press unit to media contacts

Remember the media show you carefully set up in sync #26? It is presently time to pitch your story to these individuals. But since you just have a single shot to establish a connection, you should contribute them a powerful manner.

Here's an awful pitch (and it frequently happens):

Hi,

I am John I might want to demand for you to compose an anecdote about our forthcoming crowdfunding effort called the Duet. Assuming you need I could send a data to you, and I'll be extremely appreciative to get your opinion.

Awaiting your reaction.

Thanks,

John

This is an awful pitch since 1) The correspondent has a name, and it isn't "Howdy" 2) He doesn't owe you any blessings 3) The item depiction is excessively short.. What precisely is a Duet?

When you are pitching to the media, I've observed that its generally more compelling to give them something first, before you request the blessing. It very well may be something as straightforward as a commendation about their composition. Regardless, make certain to give before you get. Additionally, remember sufficient data about your item story for the pitch email with the goal that the columnist will need to investigate further. Try not to compose an affection letter, yet don't be lethargic as well. Invest in some opportunity to work on composing your pitch as briefly as possible.

Here's an incredible format that you can follow:

Subject Title: re: 20 free Coolest Cooler giveaways

[Reporter's first name] - meeting you's extraordinary. I honestly love [Primary Website Domain] and needed to pass on something new that could be a great fit for your open air party gear area. I've appended a picture of the Coolest Cooler outside party box. Our Kickstarter page has a video and list items on for what reason is unique.

We figure Coolest Cooler could be an incredible story for [Primary Website Name] for these reasons:

Innovative 3-in-1 box - Coolest Cooler is the world's first party box camouflaged as a cooler, bringing mixed beverages, music and amusing to any outside occasion

Versatile use - The cooler box even has USB charging, in our current reality where individuals frequently run out of battery at ocean side gatherings. A charging point mounted on

a cooler box is uncommon in the industry.

Made for party individuals - Coolest Cooler is simply loaded with such a lot of good times you'll search for reasons to get outside more often.

If you're intrigued, if it's not too much trouble, let me in on how I can make the creative cycle simple for your group. I'm glad to join these hello there res photographs (YOUR PR KIT URL LINK HERE)

We've likewise recognized 50 party forces to be reckoned with comprised of ocean side DJs, columnists and bloggers to approach for surveys. You're one of them. We will offer 10 sets for an audit. Could you like a couple to audit? Tell me! We send off December 10 at 9am PST.

Thanks for investing in some opportunity

#35: Send out item tests to 10 individuals in your organization and request reviews

If you are crowdfunding an actual item, getting audits from early clients is a urgent advance. With item surveys, your mission will stand apart in light of the fact that it as of now has social proof.

The method for getting these early audits is to convey item tests. A word of caution though: if your product sample fails to function properly when the reviewers are testing it out, it can have a negative blowback effect. My startup wrongly was arrogant, and conveyed Duet tests to Techcrunch.com before we had completely tried them. Presently on the off chance that you don't have the foggiest idea, Techcrunch is the greatest tech startup blog in the world!

What happened was that our versatile application ended up being buggy, and the correspondent who tried our Duets composed a horrible article about our mission, which didn't help us in any capacity. The illustration? Guarantee item tests are completely working and without any errors before they are sent out.

Back to conveying your audit tests… Do it in two stages. Keep in mind that individuals are occupied, particularly assuming you are sending them out to bloggers. Ensure they comprehend that you anticipate nothing from them. If they are busy then they can ignore it. Assuming that they answer emphatically, send over the examples. Your outcomes will improve fundamentally. When you have the delicate responsibility from them they'll be significantly more prone to really help you.

Week 6

#36: Temporary mystery site to be ready

Once you're finished with the brief site, it is currently time to run it through with undoubtedly five others, and do a somewhat late check for missing substance, pictures, and broken links.

It is generally smart to do A/B split testing of your secret site. Essentially, you make two somewhat various forms of your site, to see which converts site guests better. At last, your objective will be for your guests to tap on the URL connect to your mission page. I recommend using Crazyegg for this purpose.

When everything is done, get a memorable simple URL that connects to your presentation page. For instance: http://www.theduet.com. The simpler it is for individuals to recall your space name, the better. Assuming that you really want a modest area name supplier, look at Bluehost.com.

#37: Continue tracking down more places to pitch your product

It's enticing to unwind and quit pitching your item now, particularly in the event that you've proactively pitched the media list before on. I know, pitching the media is likely one of the most tedious assignments in your mission, however it must be done.

If you're cold messaging the media the initial time, be arranged that just around 10% of them will at any point answer to your email. The explanation is on the grounds that these journalists would many pitches be able to like you ordinary, and it is entirely expected for them to overlook yours. To that end your pitch feature must be sufficiently attractive to warrant their attention!

That said, you would rather not take a risk with things. Your possibilities of a great answer increment as you have more news sources you can pitch to. Subsequently, it is vital to keep tracking down more weblocales, sites, and forces to be reckoned with to pitch your story to.

#38: Video to be ready

Now's an ideal opportunity to ensure your video is great. Assess the lighting, sound and embellishments (if any) once more. Dive deep, and go exceptionally point by point at this stage. In the event that the sound is excessively delicate at specific places, demand for the volume to be turned up. On the off chance that the lighting shows up too brilliant in certain scenes, explicitly record the specific time and illuminate your videographer right away. He/she shouldn't have any issues rolling out the improvements in no less than a little while circle back time.

All in, the last video ought to be prepared for feature in this week.

#39: Put together the video, composed pitch, item pictures, rewards and early surveys on the mission page

Follow your crowdfunding stage's directions on the best way to arrangement the mission page. It's essential to peruse their Terms and Conditions before you continue to put the different mission components together.

Oftentimes, crusades get dismissed even before they are sent off for exceptionally straightforward, yet frequently neglected reasons. One normal dismissal reason on Kickstarter is when project proprietors utilize 3D renderings of their items, rather than a real model for their mission graphics.

Week 7

#40: Finalize and edit the mission page

Look through the mission page once through once more, and check whether the progression of show is smooth and consistent. Additionally check through the pitch duplicate for linguistic and spelling errors.

#41: Plan your stretch goals

Stretch objectives are subsidizing targets set by project proprietors ahead of time past the first financing objectives. These extra financing objectives are in many cases delivered halfway through the undertaking and are utilized to collect more cash, to improve the prizes. Stretch objectives are best utilized related to the presentation of a new, somewhat pricier mission reward perk, as you'll require a method for increasing sell existing backers.

Some instances of stretch objectives are:

- Your item in a restricted version color
- An extra accessory
- Features that work on the general nature of your product
- A portable application that will be created for both Android and iPhone

#42: Continue tracking down more places to pitch your product

As recently talked about in #37, keep tracking down more websites, locales, and powerhouses to pitch your story to.

#43: Submit crusade for endorsement on crowdfunding stage (assuming utilizing Kickstarter)

When everything is prepared, present your mission for endorsement assuming your crowdfunding stage requires it. For Indiegogo, you don't require endorsement while for Kickstarter, it could take anyplace between 48-72 hours for your undertaking to be supported, dependent upon their terms and conditions.

So factor in a cradle season of somewhere around 3 days if going the Kickstarter course. Likewise, you will need to keep an extra week as a 'cradle' to test-drive your campaign.

Week 8

#44: Make any last changes to your crowdfunding effort page

This is the week to test-drive your mission after your mission is endorsed. Insofar as you don't click 'send off project' yet, both Kickstarter and Indiegogo will permit you to send a review connect to others, so you can get their input and make changes.

Most of the time, you'll get feedbacks such as "I think you need to include a picture here' or "Your pricing is too expensive". These early criticism is entirely significant, and you ought to rapidly make a move once you get them.

#45: Continue tracking down more places to pitch your product

As recently talked about in #37, keep tracking down more web journals, locales, and powerhouses to pitch your story to.

#46: Take a little while off to rest (you'll have to get ready for the following period of your campaign)

For now, require a little while off to rest and be revived, in light of the fact that the following lap will be considerably really testing (however energizing)! You'll have to recapture the energy and concentration to run the most elating mile of the whole mission: the genuine launch!

Week 9

#47: Take a full breath and press "Launch!"

Launching your mission interestingly can be a seriously exciting, yet terrifying inclination. Inside, you likely are anxious to see that first vow. Then again, you could likewise get apprehensive and keep thinking about whether any vows would even come in whatsoever, or on the other hand assuming the mission would hit its goal.

If you can relate to these sentiments, cheer up that I was once from your perspective as well. At the point when we sent off the Duet project on April

5, we had no clue about what's in store. Would we be able to try and cross our $5,000 objective? Could patrons like our item? What would it be advisable for me to do straightaway? This multitude of fears hid to me as I tapped the 'Send off Campaign' button.

It would have helped enormously in the event that someone could come close by to guarantee me that I was doing great after the mission send off. Fortunately for you, we'll take a gander at the right strides for you to take after you've launched.

#48: Back your own mission if conceivable (Kickstarter doesn't permit this however) and back the most elevated conceivable vow level you can afford

Before you raise any assets, it is best if you would initially contribute assets to your own undertaking first. 'Canine fooding' is the term authored to depict evaluating your own items first on yourself, prior to offering it to other people. It is great to do this since you really show that you put stock in your item. It is prescribed to back your most expensive bundle, to give your vows a huge lift. Relax, you'll in any case in the long run get back the vast majority of your vow, less the crowdfunding stage fees.

#49: If you have a group, inspire them to back promises as well. (Make sure to discount them later on.)

If you have a group working all day with you on the task, inspire them to contribute too to the venture and deal them a refund or organization benefit. Some crowdfunding stages, like Indiegogo, permit you to do this as they are really careless on where the financing sources come from. Remember however, that Kickstarter doesn't permit commitments from your own accounts.

#50: Send customized messages to 20-30 of your family and dear companions and request that they assist with kicking off your mission

On send off day, distinguish 20-30 of your nearest loved ones who realize you well, and send a customized email to every one of them to request their assistance to kick off your mission. Try not to convey an overall email to them, as doing so will do nothing to fortify the relationship. An email addressed to 'Aunt Anne' will be significantly more powerful, than 'Dear Family'.

Something like:

It's that short and basic: only four segments and directly forthright. It has been demonstrated endlessly time once more, that customized messages are better. This is on the grounds that individuals are more averse to accomplish something when asked collectively than when they are asked independently. Everyone feels that another person will venture forward to help first. So in the event that you cc-ed Auntie Anne in an overall email with all your other relatives, odds are she won't take action.

#51: Announce the send off on all your/and your group's online entertainment networks

Now's an ideal opportunity to be improper and effectively advance your mission interface all over! You ought to report the send off of your mission in all the social
media networks that you are a piece of. At the absolute minimum, you ought to declare your mission in Facebook, Twitter and Google+.

However, remember that having 10000 devotees on these organizations doesn't liken to promises. Furthermore, there are a lot of not so genuine outsider administrations that offer you the choice to purchase thousands, and even great many supporters on Facebook and Twitter.

So it is really not about the numbers. It is about how many *engaged* followers you have, who will actually support and share your campaign. 100 engaged followers on Twitter are worth much more than 100000 Twitter fans that aren't engaged. If you don't already have a crowd of engaged audience, you can still spend time building a following. But do remember that growing a community takes time and lots of effort, and it won't happen overnight, and you'll have to continue posting a variety of content (videos, announcements, helpful tips etc.) throughout the campaign. If you do not have the time or resources to handle this, then do consider hiring a community manager to do it for you.

I would say, online entertainment networks are best utilized as an instrument to immediately spread expression of your mission extensively. On the off chance that you can bear to financial plan in Facebook Ads, its an especially fast and powerful method for getting familiarity with your mission before large number of eyeballs.

But here's an expression of wariness. Try not to depend on Facebook, Twitter nor Google+ as an essential wellspring of change into vows. Recollect that the principle reason individuals hang out via web-based entertainment destinations for finding their companions lives, not to see notices! So it is simply sensible to expect extremely low change rates.

#52: Announce the send off on all internet based networks you're in

Do not neglect to report your mission send off in the gathering/conversation bunches that you're in too!

Ideally, when of the mission send off, you ought to as of now have been a functioning supporter and member in these discussions. Try to contribute something of significant worth first in quite a while, to develop validity. And only much later do you share your campaign link. Most discussions will be exceptionally able to permit you to post your mission connect, insofar as you don't seem to be spammy.

#53: Announce the send off on interface destinations/crowdfunding list sites

Another extraordinary road to advance your crowdfunding effort is to submit it on crowdfunding join locales. Remember that these are local area sites, bloggers and discussions, and they are controlled by genuine individuals. Individuals can see when you really do truly think often about the local area or simply need promises. On the off chance that you have the outlook to really lay out connections all things being equal, you'll have higher possibilities of success.

Here are some crowdfunding locales you can present your campaign:

- Crowdfundingforum
- KickingItForward
- Ayudos
- Kickstarterforum

Google+ Groups
- Crowdfunding
- Kickstarter Supporters And Campaigns
- Crowdfunding Hub
- Kickstarters

It is energetically suggested that you present your official statement article, rather than an immediate mission interface without help from anyone else, which enhances the community.

#54: Send a send off email to your mailing list

Up to this point, you have your email list endorsers amped up for the approaching send off of your mission. It is currently time to send them an email declaring that your mission has at last launched.

Building energy and expectation in your email list about the send off of your crowdfunding effort is a craftsmanship in itself. Some time before you even send off, guarantee that you've arranged and set up a succession of messages that will illuminate your supporters on the specific date you're mission will go live, so they have the opportunity. Try not to just 'trap' your endorsers with one deals email on send off day. All in all, how often do you purchase an item following catching wind of it for the first time?

Be certain to incorporate an exceptional impetus to your email endorsers, to make it more straightforward for them to back you. Restricted timely riser loads of your item, or an extra advantage tossed in are only two of the numerous compelling ways of inspiring them to take out their wallets.

There are a lot of content and material worked out there that arrangement with email showcasing exhaustively. Nathan Barry has written a very extensive article on product launches here that will help you: <u>How To Launch Anything</u>

#55: Send your first mission update to thank your initial sponsor on Day 1

From day 1, your supporters ought to feel that you and your group are real and generally present, so remember to thank your initial patrons. Most crowdfunding stages have "Another this Week" or "As of late Launched" projects segment, and these can be extremely helpful to drive in introductory vows. So thank these patrons, and furthermore give them basic means to impart your mission to their friends.

#56: Inform media list that your mission is alive

You've endeavored to educate the press about the send off regarding your mission. This present time's the opportunity to refresh them that your mission's sent off! Drop them an email, and obviously it doesn't damage to remind them with a short review of what's going on with's your mission, along with your mission interface too.

#57: Give yourself a congratulatory gesture toward the finish of the week

Phew! It's been a truly rushed first seven day stretch of send off. Grab a seat toward the week's end and give yourself a congratulatory gesture for a wonderful piece of handiwork! Little dosages of consolation go far to keep you in the race.

#58: Set up an every minute of every day schedule with your group to look after your mission (optional)

You ought to screen your mission's remarks segment nonstop, day in and day out. The explanation is on the grounds that you would rather not permit any an open door for a solitary de-useful or pessimistic remark to appear in the remarks segment, and snowball into objections and most exceedingly terrible, refunds.

As your task advances, you'll need to keep up with associations with a many individuals. You'll start to invest more energy noting remarks, client assistance messages, as well as distributorship and PR enquiries. This can rapidly get overpowering and turned into your principle center, on first spot on your list of fundamental things to do.

I observe that it pays to set up a group program to alternate to watch the remark area, or undertaking somebody to deal with these client service exercises promptly.

#59: Send a second mission update to patrons about your task's progress

For the second mission update, I'd recommend you to address any Frequently Asked Questions (FAQs) that your supporters could have. Being a brand new project, it's highly likely that there'll be areas of your campaign that your backers will still need further clarification. This is a fun opportunity to answer their questions.

Week 10

*Note: now, assuming you've done everything referenced in the earlier week yet have not figured out how to raise something like 30% of your subsidizing objective; it ought to act as an unmistakable risk sign to you. You are either not hustling to the point of getting more mindfulness, or individuals most likely don't see a need to leave behind their well deserved cash for your venture. I suggest that you return to the past advances and check whether you've missed anything, or kill the mission early and assess what turned out badly to save time and effort.

After all, crowdfunding is a round of high gamble. Here and there you win enormous, and at times you gain from your mistakes.

#60: Follow up on media contacts/press in the event that they have not answered you yet

If your media contacts have not answered you, a basic short update email like: "Hello Jim, simply checking. *.did you end up accepting my past email last week?" will get the job done the majority of the time.*

I've given this a shot myself while pitching media and frequently observe that the correspondents are essentially excessively occupied. But if you send in a follow up email, they are much more inclined to reply to your request.

#61: Continue posting a combination of content on friendly media

Maintaining a virtual entertainment presence is vital for individuals to realize you are 'there'. But the amount of work that goes into preparing your crowdfunding campaign is crazily heavy. It is a migraine to continuously be finding and posting new happy on Facebook/Twitter.

I suggest that you evaluate Beatrix. Beatrix is a virtual entertainment colleague apparatus, and it is adequately shrewd to source and distribute important online entertainment refreshes for you without you expecting to lift a finger.

#62: Handle any potential patron enquiries

Reply supporter enquiries instantly when they remark on your campaign page. You're likewise probable get a couple private messages from possible supporters, rather than seeing their messages in the remarks segment. The justification behind this is on the grounds that Kickstarter and Indiegogo manages just permit patrons who have promised to post remarks in the mission page.

#63: Continue observing the remarks segment closely

Running a crowdfunding effort is an every minute of every day activity, as your benefactors come from various timezones. That doesn't mean you don't require rest for those 30 days, however you'll in any case must have a method for observing new remarks and answer as fast as possible. During available time, set an objective of answering back inside 15minutes, while after available time, consider having your group pivot and alternate to screen the comments.

#64: Send a third mission update to backers

You could send supporters a third mission update on your assembling and delivery progress. Show them photos of your industrial facility or office, and furthermore let them know how might you be turning out transportation and conveyance to get your item to them.

#65: Introduce your first stretch objective (if needed)

If energy has been fabricating great, this is a happy chance to present your stretch objective. Stretch objectives regularly work best when you as of now have a sensible measure of footing, and a sizeable base of backers.

Week 11

#66: Send a fourth mission challenge update to urge supporters to allude friends

I think running a reference challenge is an incredible method for activating your current sponsor to allude companions to your mission. With the right motivators, reference challenges can be an extremely viable method for inspiring your benefactors to get a new increase in vows. Eventually, be all around as inventive as conceivable while arranging reference contests.

#67: Post a mid-crusade advantage to up-sell backers

A typical example frequently happens halfway through any crowdfunding effort. Deals begin to dial back to a stream, and it tends to be very difficult to get new sponsor in.

A cure to this is acquaint an exceptional advantage with upsell your current patrons. This advantage ought to be valued higher than your fundamental advantage bundle. You may be astonished that individuals really do truly need to pay something else for a more costly reward!

#68: Post a video update

A video update to your sponsor now would be an invigorating break from the standard text refreshes they've been getting. Maybe record a video of you and your group, and show your benefactors what you've really depend on at the workplace. Think about showing the lighter side of things in the group, similar to a meeting of each colleague and his/her interests.

Weird as it might sound, yet your sponsor would like to know that you're human too!

#69: Introduce your second stretch objective (if needed)

If you figured out how to hit your past stretch objective, you can proceed to acquaint a second stretch objective with urge more benefactors to promise to your project.

#70: Continue circle back to media contacts/press

As examined in sync #60.

#71: Continue posting a combination of content on friendly media

As talked about in sync #61.

#72: Continue observing the remarks area closely

As examined in sync #63.

Week 12

#73: Send a fifth mission update to remind your supporters why you are running this project

By the fourth and last seven day stretch of your mission, I can nearly promise you: a portion of your first patrons would have failed to remember what your mission was all about.

As your mission attracts to a nearby, send them an update that helps them the story to remember how your item happened, and say thanks to them for putting into your vision.

#74: Continue circle back to media contacts/press

As examined in sync #60.

#75: Continue checking the remarks segment closely

As talked about in sync #63.

#76: Continue posting a combination of content on friendly media

As examined in sync #61.

#77: Introduce your third stretch objective (if needed)

This is the last push! You can present your third (or more) stretch objective here to revitalize your patrons for one last push to the completion line!

#78: Collect the cash, and try to compensate yourself!

If you've come to this progression, CONGRATULATIONS! You've come to the end goal, following a tiresome 90 days. Ideally you have likewise figured out how to hit your subsidizing objective. Regardless of whether you hit your objective, cheer up on the grounds that the abundance of involvement and information you've acquired is extremely valuable, and can be re-applied to an ensuing crowdfunding campaign.

Allow around 5 working days for Kickstarter or Indiegogo to move the assets raised to your ledger. Meanwhile, kick back your shoes and enjoy some time off! Invest energy with your loved ones. Go out to a pleasant supper. Be glad that you've accomplished something the vast majority just wanted to do.